If Giving Is Not It:

Joyful Living Through Giving

Nita
Thanks for your
life of giving.

Claude Robold

written by
Claude L. Robold

II Corinthians 8:7 NIV

Acknowledgements

It is with great appreciation that I say thank you to Executive Mentor, Bobb Biehl. He has taught me many important processes. He encouraged me early in our relationship to write a book. Now finally, I have ventured into that arena. Thank you, Bobb, for consistently saying, "Write a book."

Also, I am greatly appreciative to Heidi Arnold for her work in editing this book. She has been a great help and encouragement to this endeavor. Her work helps make this book possible.

Years ago, a lady sketched a drawing for me in appreciation of what she had received through our ministry. Today that drawing, with her permission, is on the cover of this book. Thank you, Cheryl Swart.

Every person mentioned in this book has proven there is joy in giving. I thank each of them for their example.

I am so thankful for the gift of abundant life and the promise of eternal life that Jesus has provided for me. I encourage everyone to receive this precious gift.

Dedication

This book is dedicated to my parents, Russell and Betty Robold who shared their lives with many—giving of themselves to enrich the lives of others. I am thankful for their legacy of giving.

Foreword

In your heart of hearts (where no one else sees), how do you honestly feel about giving? No, really. How do you feel about giving of your time, energy, and money?

In this one, clearly written book, Claude brings 21 inspiring perspectives on giving! This book—addressing a joyful life through giving—is not just a subject with my friend, Claude Robold, but a way of life. I have witnessed Claude's own lifestyle of giving in various ways to enrich the lives of others. His generosity of time, energy, and his own resources to develop leaders on a global scale qualifies him to tell these stories that we should consider as examples in our own life.

You will discover that Claude does not brag about his own giving but lifts from the lives of others the joy found in the many ways of giving far beyond monetary means. You will be reminded of the many ways your own life has been inspired to give by the models of others as they have given generously into your life. The biblical accounts on giving will remind all of us that it is truly a blessing to live a life of joyful giving. You will be challenged to join in this wonderful life quest of spreading joy through giving. As you know, this is a great need in our global society today.

Bobb Biehl—Coach, Consultant, Executive Mentor, writer and lifelong friend of Claude and Jan Robold

Introduction

This book came about as I pondered a statement my father, Russell A. Robold, shared with me about what he thought was important in life after having served for over 60 years. He said, "If giving is not it, I missed it altogether."

At this writing, he has now been gone for 16 years. Yet those words linger in my mind. As I pondered his response, I began to recall how many examples of giving I have seen through the lives and experiences of others. I am sharing 21 of those stories. The number of stories could go higher, but I have chosen these to help us see a broad scope in giving.

I have written them as I remember them with the purpose to "spur us on to love and good deeds, encouraging others all the more." It is my desire these 21 days of reading, reflecting, and writing will encourage you in the life of giving. I want each of you to know the joy of living through giving. If we each grow in our capacity to give, our world will be a richer place and many lives will be not only blessed but transformed. You will find giving is transformational for the giver and the recipient.

May the blessings of giving be yours,

Claude L. Robold

How to Use This Book

This book has been designed to not only share stories, insights, and principles of living, but a joyful life through giving. I desire that as you read, reflect, and study that your own stories, insights, and principles will come to mind. I have, therefore, provided a page at the end of each chapter for you to begin to record your personal reflections.

I have said this book provides a way to discover and renew joyful living through giving in 21 days. You could use this book for 21 weeks versus 21 days, making each chapter a time of receiving, reflecting, and creating your joyful path to giving. This will allow you more time to reflect on the biblical passages and write out your stories of giving.

You could also provide others the opportunity to enjoy their journey of joyful living through giving by gifting a copy of this book. You may purchase copies on Amazon.

Table of Contents

If Giving Is Not It,
I Missed It Altogether

The warm spring day had invited us outdoors. My father and I were enjoying the warm fresh air and the beauty of spring. My father was in his late 70s and semi-retired from full-time pastoral ministry. He had moved to Middletown, Ohio, to assist me in the ministry at New Covenant Church.

As we visited, I was listening to learn of some of his memorable times in ministry. I raised the question, "Dad, what was your major highlight in the 50 plus years of your ministry?" He quickly replied, "If giving isn't it, then I missed it altogether?" I was at first surprised at the answer, but as I began to review in my mind the life of my father, I knew he had not missed it.

He was a giver. He had given the early years of his life to the United States military serving in the Second World War as a radioman and rear gunner in a B-17. He flew over 35 missions in the European Theater during the war.

Not long after his honorable discharge from the military, he found his way back to Christ. This moment when he gave his life to Christ in a local Church of God in Muncie, Indiana, continued a journey of giving, but now for the honor of Christ. He would soon enter the ministry and became a pastor. He gave the rest of his life to building up local churches to advance the Kingdom of God.

When he was 79, he announced to me that he was leaving Middletown to accept the pastorate of the Church of God in Crawfordsville, Indiana—once again giving himself to the call of God. He shared with me that his financial package in Crawfordsville was the largest he had ever received in 50 years of ministry. He was now living from a pension. Therefore, he took his weekly income from the church in Crawfordsville and sent it to a young pastor in a struggling work. He did this for the three years he was in Crawfordsville. The Lord blessed his work, and 15 men came to accept Jesus as their Lord in his short time with the church. NO! He did not miss it at all. Giving is what life is all about.

The following writings are stories from the lives of people who learned the art of giving. They are a part of the Kingdom of God and realized God had given His only son that they might have life abundantly and eternally. They lived lives that bear witness to the blessing of giving.

Principle:
You Cannot Outgive God

Reflection

- Who in your life comes to mind when you think about givers?

- What did you learn from their example?

- How would you describe your giving?

- What do you aspire to give in your lifetime?

"Give and it will be given to you. A good measure pressed down, shaken together, and running over, it will be poured into your lap. For with the measure you use, it will be measured to you." Luke 6:38

Apply the 3-10-1 method: Read the verse three times, summarize its meaning in 10 words or less, and ask God to reveal one thing He wants to communicate to you.

Dig Deeper: Read the context. Luke 6:27-42

Personal Insights & Reflection

---><>·<·<o<<<---

Giving Because You Care

I was five years of age when my father, Russell Robold, accepted a call to become the pastor of the Church of God in Tyler, Texas. This was quite a move from Muncie. As a young boy, I do not remember a lot of the people in the congregation, but I do recall Mrs. Dixon. She was a schoolteacher. She was more of a grandmother figure from my point of view. She dressed nicely and seemed to me in my young appraisal to have some wealth. It was the year 1950, and Mrs. Dixon was the owner of a brand new 1950 Plymouth sedan.

It was in 1950 that my father would lose the last living parent in his life. Emily Robold had been battling breast cancer. The medical field in those days did not have the advancements now available to us. I recall visiting in her home just before she passed. She seemed to be in a lot of pain and worried in particular about one of her nine sons. She felt he was far from God and kept calling for him.

This visit was made possible by a generous gift of a lady who we barely knew. Yes, Mrs. Dixon. My family did not have an automobile that was worthy of making the long trip from Texas to Indiana. I am not sure how it came about. Mrs. Dixon came to my father and offered the use of her brand-new car for the trip. My father resisted by saying, "It is your brand-new car." She replied with, "That is why you should take it on this trip." I have remembered this story all my life as an example that whatever we have is just a tool afforded us to use and bless others.

The story is highlighted by an unfortunate event. While my father was visiting his dying mother in her home, Mrs. Dixon's new 1950 Plymouth was parked in front of the house of my grandmother, Emily Robold. The clothes my family had brought for the trip were hanging in the car. During this time, someone broke into the car and stole all their clothing.

I later learned that when they returned home to Tyler, people in the church bought my father a new suit to replace the one that had been stolen. My mother was a seamstress, so they took her shopping and paid for enough fabric material for her to sew herself two new outfits.

Givers are people who bless others with that which they have been blessed. After all, it all belongs to the Lord.

Principle:
All I Have Comes Through the Hand of God; Therefore, God Has the Right to Request Use of It

Reflection

- Who in your life stepped up in a time of need and blessed you or your family?
- Beyond the tangible gift, what did you receive from their act of giving?
- When was the last time you met a tangible need in someone's life?
- Who in your circle of influence may be in need?
- What could you do to help meet the need?

"The earth is the Lord's, and everything in it, the world, and all who live in it." Psalm 24:1

Apply the 3-10-1 method: Read the verse three times, summarize its meaning in 10 words or less, and ask God to reveal one thing He wants to communicate to you.

Dig Deeper: Read the context. Psalm 24

Personal Insights & Reflection

THE CHRISTMAS TOFFEE

The small town of Fairmount, Indiana, has two citizens of notoriety: the actor James Dean and the author of the cartoon Garfield, Jim Davis. I knew neither of them, yet I too was a resident of the small town. It was here I entered the first grade and I recall my teachers being Mrs. Anderson, first grade; Mrs. Patterson, second grade; and Mrs. Fife, third grade. Although I have distinct memories of them related to stories of my time under their tutelage, it is a person whose name I do not know that I most remember for his generosity.

He was the owner of the local lumberyard which was two blocks from my home in Fairmount. This was my father's second pastorate, a small congregation of the Church of God where he was paid $25 a week for his full-time position. It was at Christmastime that I remember the first act of giving by the gentleman who owned the lumberyard. He gave to our family a five-pound box of chocolate-covered toffee.

I was thrilled when I had a few pennies to stop by the local gas station and buy a package of Kit Kats, a favorite package of four small pieces of candy. Wow! When I saw this five-pound box of candy setting on the coffee table in our living room, I thought, who has that much money to buy such a large box of candy, and why would he give it to us? He did not even go to our church. As a small boy, I was impressed.

His second gift of generosity was even greater. The Church of God had bought a church building from the Episcopal church. It was a stately building with stained glass windows and a tall steeple. However, the early leaders of the Church of God thought the stained-glass windows and the steeple were worldly symbols of opulence and replaced all the windows and removed the steeple. After pastoring the church for two years, my father thought the steeple ought to be replaced. He went to the lumberyard to price the cost of lumber to build the frame for the steeple. When the owner of the lumberyard heard of the intent to replace the steeple, he shared with my father that years ago when the original steeple had been removed, he had placed money in a bank account so that when anyone would want to rebuild the steeple there would be funds to do so. It was not his church but the steeple with a spire and cross at the top was a symbol of Christianity to the community, and he wanted it to rise skyward again.

Today in Fairmount the steeple still rises to the sky to declare the glory of God. My father engraved these words on the cross that tops the steeple: I'm going higher someday.

We never know who is watching what we do and is willing to give to make it possible. There are individuals who desire to make good things happen. The candy toffee was good, but it is gone. The cross rises high into the sky calling to all: this is where we were all set free.

Principle:
Givers Have Ways of Sharing
a Good and Lasting Message

Reflection

- Who gave a gift in your life that has left a lasting impression?

- Who is in need in your circle of influence that a gift from you might make a lifelong impression?

"Whoever sows sparingly will also reap sparingly, and whoever sows generously will also reap generously." 2 Corinthians 9:6

Apply the 3-10-1 method: Read the verse three times, summarize its meaning in 10 words or less, and ask God to reveal one thing He wants to communicate to you.

Dig Deeper: Read the context. II Corinthians 9:1-15

Personal Insights & Reflection

The Care of an Older Giver

Her name was Mary Rice. She and her husband were pioneer ranchers on the outskirts of the western Oklahoma town known as Elk City. When I was in the fourth grade, our family moved from Fairmount, Indiana, to Elk City, Oklahoma where my father accepted the pastorate of the First Church of God.

This move had taken us far away from any family members. My grandparents on my mother's side were my only living grandparents, and they resided in Indiana. To say the move was a culture shock would be putting it mildly.

Mary was now a widow. She had four grown sons, Hillary, Herschel and Eugene, who had all become ministers and James was a rancher. This quickly gives you the insight that Mary's home was a Godly home. She was one of the prayer warriors of the church.

She became for me and my sisters our surrogate grandmother. Not long after we moved to Elk City, she asked my parents if she could have me and my sisters at her home for a few hours every other Saturday. This became a delightful practice for the next three years.

Mary would warmly welcome us into her home where the aroma of fresh baked cookies filled the air. She would have ready for us a Dr. Pepper, ice cream and fresh baked cookies. After the delightful treat, she would always have us help clean up the glasses and dishes. She would then take us into her back sun porch during the warm months of the year and her front room during the winter. There she would read to us from the Bible and share an experience from the scriptures and then have prayer with us. We could stay as long as we wanted, but when it came time to leave, she always had a freshly baked cake for us to take home for the family.

After I was grown and had entered the ministry, I was invited to hold a series of services at the Elk City church. Mary Rice requested the pastor to allow me to stay in her home during those days. It was a wonderful remembrance and a fresh time of prayer with Mary. If someone did for you what Mary did for our family, may you find ways to return the blessing or pass it on to another.

Principle:
Regardless of Age, You Have Something to Give

Reflection

- Who was the elderly person that invested in your life?

- What difference did their investment make in your life?

- Who in the generations under you need a giving touch from you?

Each one should use whatever gift he has received to serve others."
I Peter 4:10a

Apply the 3-10-1 method: Read the verse three times, summarize its meaning in 10 words or less, and ask God to reveal one thing He wants to communicate to you.

Dig Deeper: Read the context. I Peter 4:7-11

Personal Insights & Reflection

Giving the Gift of Prophecy

I was a 10-year-old fifth grader living in Elk City, and I had never seen a hand as big as his. Rev. Mitchell was the evangelist for a series of meetings in the church my father was pastoring. The meetings extended through a two-week period.

During that time, we came to know the evangelist loved fishing. He and my father went to Clinton Lake to fish a couple of times while he was leading the meetings.

It was Saturday morning and the meetings had concluded on that Friday evening. The evangelist had stopped at our home to say goodbye to my father before returning to his home in Midwest City, Oklahoma. He had parked his car along the curb near our front yard. I had accompanied him and my father as they walked toward his car.

The evangelist went to the trunk of his car and opened it where you could see an array of fishing gear. He pulled out a fishing rod and reel and walked over and handed it to me, and said, "Here, enjoy fishing with your dad." Then he placed his huge hand on the top of my head and said, "One day you will be a fisher of men." He had just given me the gift of a word of prophecy.

I can only remember fishing twice with my father, and I never caught anything. However, I never forgot the word of prophecy. The summer of my 18th year I was having lunch with my father. He looked at me from the other end of the table and asked, "Are you ready to sell your car and enroll at Gulf Coast Bible College to study for ministry?" I immediately replied," Yes sir!" Thus began my journey of being a fisher of men and to this day I continue.

I am forever grateful for the gift of prophecy from long ago. I have always been aware of 10-year-old young boys and girls and the call that God may have upon their lives.

May you, as God prompts, give a word of encouragement to some young life in which you see the hand of God working.

Principle:

Speaking a Word of Prophecy Is Affirming What You See God Doing in the Life of Another

Reflection

- What person spoke into your life?

- What do their words mean to you today?

- What work of God do you see taking place in the life of another?

- Will you affirm it?

"Let us consider how we may spur one another on toward love and good deeds." Hebrews 10:24

Apply the 3-10-1 method: Read the verse three times, summarize its meaning in 10 words or less, and ask God to reveal one thing He wants to communicate to you.

Dig Deeper: Read the context. Hebrews 10: 19-25

Personal Insights & Reflection

You Can't Outgive God

I was but 14 years old when I learned you cannot outgive God. I had worked mowing lawns during the summer. As we approached mid-summer, it was time to go to youth camp. That week I had earned $5 mowing five lawns. I worked cheap in those days. My parents had taught me the biblical principle of tithing 10% of what you earn belongs to God.

As I was sitting in church on the Sunday we would leave for camp, I had my 50 cents ready to put in the offering plate—my tithe for the week. I began to think what that extra 50 cents would purchase at the camp snack bar or the craft table. I was debating on whether to keep the tithe for myself. However, as the offering plate passed me, I gave God what was his and placed the tithe in the offering plate.

That afternoon we were gathering to go to youth camp. As I was preparing to get in the car for the trip, one of the men of the church, a local businessman, Leonard Laurner, approached me. He put forward his hand as to shake hands with me saying; "Have a great time at camp." As I clutched his hand, he placed something in my hand. It was a five-dollar bill. He said, "I thought you could use some spending money at camp." Yep, you guessed it! You can't outgive God.

I have continued to be a tither and giver from that day to this. I have experienced the truth that if your hands are open to God so he can take anything out, they are also open so that he can put anything in your hand he desires. I have found that He puts more in my hand than He takes out.

I dare you to trust God with your giving and watch the blessings flow. God honors obedient and cheerful givers.

Principle:
There Is Abundance in Being an Open-Handed Steward

Reflection

- Mr. Laurner was a tither, but he was also a giver. You really give nothing from your resources until you give beyond the tithe.

- Who would be abundantly blessed if you gave beyond your tithe?

"Bring the whole tithe into the storehouse, that there may be food in my house. Test me in this, says the Lord Almighty, and see if I will not throw open the floodgates of heaven and pour out so much blessing that you will not have room enough for it." Malachi 3:10

Apply the 3-10-1 method: Read the verse three times, summarize its meaning in 10 words or less, and ask God to reveal one thing He wants to communicate to you.

Dig Deeper: Read the context. Malachi 3:7-12

Personal Insights & Reflection

You Never Know Who Has What to Give

We were starting New Covenant Church in the year 1987. Our beginnings were meager. A local church had loaned us for free a chapel building in which to begin the church. As a new church, we were so happy with this chapel that had an upper and lower level.

Not long after we had begun services in the chapel, one of the ladies of this new church who was a single mom worked cleaning houses and running a fruit stand in the summer. Donna Bryant was a cheerful soul. She had endured a lot of difficulty in life, but she had the joy of the Lord in her soul.

She said, "Pastor, I do not have a lot of money to give but if you would allow me, I would like to clean the chapel each week for free as my gift to God." Naturally we accepted her offer. I would often be in the office of the chapel when she was cleaning. You could always hear Donna singing a song of joy as she was cleaning.

I should have guessed from the beginning that Donna was a giver. Several years later, New Covenant had purchased land and built their first building, a multiple-purpose worship center. Donna carried her cleaning commitment over to the new building even though it was much larger than the chapel. She kept this commitment until illness stopped her from being able to work any longer. She had an extended battle with cancer which ended in her ultimate reward of heaven.

Several months after Donna went to be with the Lord, I received a call from an attorney. She asked if Donna Bryant had been a member of our congregation. I affirmed that she had been until her passing. She then introduced herself as Donna's attorney and told me that Donna had put New Covenant Church in her will. She had left us her home and the adjoining property. I was astonished.

You never know who God is going to bless and use as a giver in His Kingdom. We would ultimately sell the property and use the proceeds for partial funding of a Family Life Center for the New Covenant Church family. Each time I would enter the Family Life Center, I would think of Donna and sometimes, in my head, I would hear her singing her songs of joy.

Principle:
Give All You Give as Unto the Lord

Reflection

- How will God use you as a cheerful giver?

- What have you given in life that is not quantified by dollars and cents?

- What gift of time or energy could you bless another person with this month?

"Each one should give what he has decided in his heart to give, not reluctantly or under compulsion, for God loves a cheerful giver."
II Corinthians 9:7

Apply the 3-10-1 method: Read the verse three times, summarize its meaning in 10 words or less, and ask God to reveal one thing He wants to communicate to you.

Dig Deeper: Read the context. II Corinthians 9

Personal Insights & Reflection

The Blessing of Family Giving

I have realized that givers usually have a partner involved in their giving. This has often been proven to be the giver's spouse. It is a blessing to see couples so united in how they use their resources to effectively give.

Donna Bryant was not the only individual who assisted in making the Family Life Center of New Covenant Church possible. On one occasion I received a call from Jim Prushing. Jim was requesting a meeting. He shared that he and his wife, Jayne, wanted to talk with me, and the subject was a good one.

The day came for our meeting, and Jim and his wife Jayne entered my office. Jim was carrying a briefcase. They started by sharing how New Covenant church had been a blessing to them and their family. They then moved the conversation to the dream we had of building the Family Life Center for New Covenant.

Jim stated they had a gift they would like to give to kick off the funding of the Family Life Center. He then reached down and lifted his briefcase and pulled out a few papers. He handed me shares of stock worth $15,000. He then asked if this would help get us started? I said, "It certainly will be a big help." He then reached back into his brief case and pulled out a few more papers. I noticed on Jayne's face a huge smile of joy. I thought, wow! These folks like to give. He then handed me additional shares of stock worth $10,000. Yes, a $25,000 gift from this couple who loved to give.

The gift was a tremendous blessing and got us started toward our dream. However, I will never forget the joy on both of their faces as they gave this gift. It was evident to me this had been covered in prayer and discussion and had been a joint agreement of what they wanted to do for the church and the Lord.

It is a blessing to give, but I believe it is a double blessing when you and your spouse, business partner, or friend join to give as a team.

Principle:
Giving With a Partner
Is a Double Blessing

Reflection

- What couple or family poured into your life or dream and became a double blessing?

- Who could you partner with to give as a team to doubly bless another?

- Who is on your team of giving?

"Do not forget to entertain strangers, for by so doing some people have entertained angels without knowing it." Hebrews 13:2.

Apply the 3-10-1 method: Read the verse three times, summarize its meaning in 10 words or less, and ask God to reveal one thing He wants to communicate to you.

Dig Deeper: Read the context. Hebrews 13: 1-6

Personal Insights & Reflection

The Neophyte Giver

It was a call I never wanted to receive. The call came late at night on a warm summer evening in June of 1973 from a lady who had recently begun attending the church. She was in tears. She spoke hysterically between sobs, "My husband is on the front porch with a gun in his lap threatening to kill himself. Can you come and help us?" Should I have called the police? Probably!

However, this family was on the edge of eternal decisions. Their teenage daughter had come to the church at the invitation of a friend. She had given her life to the Lord. The change in her life was so evident that her mother had started attending the church. Her father had been a few times.

As I arrived at their home that night, I could see the silhouette of the man sitting on the steps to his house. As I approached him, I could see the gun laying at his side. Lord, I said, "I need your help." The gentleman greeted me with words I did not expect. "Hi Pastor, good to see you." The conversation opened with a willing heart to hear. That evening instead of taking his life, he accepted life from Jesus.

35

In the weeks ahead, I would baptize the entire family. They began to attend the church regularly and dive into growing by being discipled. It was during this time the church was going through a few struggles financially. The income was not matching the outgo. We were holding $18,000 of unpaid invoices. We had cut the budget to the bone, and this was at a pivotal moment in the life of this resurging church.

I asked the Lord for direction, and I believe he gave me the plan called Miracle 18. I was to call the church to pray for a month on what God would have them give above their regular tithes and offerings to meet the need for a special offering of clearing the $18,000 worth of invoices. The church readily joined in the plan for prayer and giving.

Miracle 18 Sunday arrived. We planned the service around this theme, and it culminated in the receiving of the miracle offering. We had a table set aside with a calculator to count the special offering right there in the service. People came forward and laid their offering on the table to be calculated. As the last gift was counted, the treasurer handed me the paper with the total. We had reached $13,100. I shared this with the congregation and gave thanks for everyone who had given and moved us toward our goal. We were a lot further down the road than when we started.

As I concluded my prayer, the new convert, who a few weeks earlier had been ready to take his life, stood and asked to speak. He began to share what the church meant to him and his family, how the church had been the lighthouse they had been looking for all their lives. He then said, "This is Miracle 18 Sunday, and the miracle is not yet complete. We need to receive another offering to complete the miracle. I am going to give an extra $1000." He walked to the table in the front of the sanctuary and wrote out the check. Others followed him, and we concluded the morning with over $20,000.

A newcomer to the faith, a neophyte in giving had led the way. I believe it was because he had been given so much by the Lord. No, not in money, but his whole family had been redeemed and given back to him. Never underestimate what people new to the faith are willing to give.

Principle:
You Do Not Have to Be
a Seasoned Giver to Begin Giving

Reflection

- Do you recall the first time you began giving? How has your giving grown?

- What person needs to hear your testimony about giving?

"But just as you excel in everything, in faith, in speech, in knowledge, see that you also excel in the grace of giving."
II Corinthians 8:7

Apply the 3-10-1 method: Read the verse three times, summarize its meaning in 10 words or less, and ask God to reveal one thing He wants to communicate to you.

Dig Deeper: Read the context. II Corinthians 8: 1-15

Personal Insights & Reflection

The Gift That Answered
a Child's Prayer

It was during our special emphasis called "Days of Refreshing" that Christian leaders from across the country came together at New Covenant Church in Middletown. This annual event proved to be most encouraging for the local church and leaders from many parts of the United States.

On one occasion Rev. Ed Davila and his wife, Olga, with their two sons traveled from San Antonio, Texas, to attend this gathering. They came in the family van. The van gave out on them just as they arrived to attend the meeting. They had the van looked at by a mechanic in the local church. They were told the problem with the van was costly, and the van was not worth investing the money.

I felt led of the Lord to share this with the congregation on the second night of the Days of Refreshing and to receive a special offering. During the evening services, we provided special programming for the children in attendance. On the same night I was sharing the need with the congregation, the Davila's young son, Eddie, was requesting prayer for a new van in the children's meeting. I was unaware of his prayer request, and he was unaware that we were taking an offering during the same time period.

The congregation and guests from around the country responded with an offering exceedingly over $8000. That evening when the Davilas were returning to their lodging in a borrowed vehicle, Olga shared with her sons that the church had given enough money through a special offering for them to get a replacement for their van.

Young Eddie responded with, "I knew he heard my prayer." Olga asked Eddie what he had prayed. He shared that he had all the children pray his family would be able to get a new car since their van was no longer useable.

The congregation responding to the prompting had given an answer to a young child's prayer. Giving always increases faith both for the giver and the receiver. Young Eddie would never forget God's answer to his prayer of faith.

Today, Eddie pastors a church in Corpus Christi, Texas. The gift of a benevolent congregation helped produce faith in a child that has produced another giving congregation.

Principle:
Never Underestimate the Prayer of a Child

Reflection

- As a child, when did you first learn the power of prayer and giving?

- What children are you encouraging in their faith development?

"If you then, though you are evil, know how to give good gifts to your children, how much more will your Father in heaven give good things to those who ask Him!" Matthew 7:11

Apply the 3-10-1 method: Read the verse three times, summarize its meaning in 10 words or less, and ask God to reveal one thing He wants to communicate to you.

Dig Deeper: Read the context. Matthew 7:7-12

Personal Insights & Reflection

Resources That Become Channels of Giving

It is amazing to me how God directs the sharing of needs to just the right people. After returning from a mission trip to India, I had the opportunity to share about building Life Centers. These centers are buildings built for local congregations for their times of worship, childcare, medical evaluations, and vocational training. You can build one of these buildings in a local village of India for the Christian community, and it gives them a platform for transforming their village. The cost of the building is $8000.

After hearing me share about these Life Centers in one of our local church services, a man by the name of Ed Collins gave me a call. He shared that he had been thinking all day about how he could build not just one Life Center but multiple Life Centers. He had just purchased another property he was preparing to rehab for rental purposes. As he had thought about this new property calculating the rehab cost, taxes, upkeep, and the rental value, he had concluded this one property would build one Life Center a year.

God had laid this on his heart, and he was going to commit this property to be his India house. Therefore, each year from henceforth, it would provide funds to build one new Life Center a year. Last I heard, the India house had been responsible for building 10 Life Centers.

We all have various resources that could become channels for giving. If we will stop and assess all that has been entrusted to us, we might find new and exciting ways to give.

I am always challenged by the question Jesus asked his disciples when he told them to feed the multitude of 5,000. They said they had no food and didn't think it wise to spend the money to feed the multitude. He replied, "What do you have? Look and see."

Perhaps this is still the challenging question to each of us. Will you look and see?

Principle:
God Uses Various Channels
to Provide Needed Resources

Reflection

- What are the various channels God has directed you to give through?

- What was one of the most unusual ways God has directed you to give?

"How many loaves do you have? Look and see." Mark 6:38a

Apply the 3-10-1 method: Read the verse three times, summarize its meaning in 10 words or less, and ask God to reveal one thing He wants to communicate to you.

Dig Deeper: Read the context. Mark 6:30-44

Personal Insights & Reflection

Givers Contribute
to Vision

S taying true to a vision or a dream that can only come to pass
if the resources are available may be one of the most difficult
tasks one faces.

Samuel Stephens asked me to walk with him to view a piece of
property the India Gospel League had purchased. As we stood
viewing the small acreage, he shared that he had a 10-year dream of
building The Carmel Conference Center on this land. The conference
center would enable the ministry to have a place to bring village
pastors to train, equip and encourage. The conference center in phase
one would be an auditorium that would house 2,200 people. Phase
two would be a large dining hall with an industrial kitchen that would
provide meals for conference attendees. Phase three would provide
lodging rooms for conference attendees. This was a 10-year vision.

Sam then asked me to join him in prayer not for the project nor the
resources to make it happen, but to pray he would be true to the
vision. He knew that phase one would cost around $250,000. He said,

"I know what that kind of money could do in the villages, and I find it difficult to stay true to the vision. Will you pray that I stay true to the vision?"

I agreed to join him in that prayer in that moment and would make it a matter of prayer in our church back in the U.S. When I returned from my trip in November of that year, I shared a report with our congregation at New Covenant Church. I told them we are not raising funds for the Carmel Conference Center but just praying Sam would remain true to the vision.

We were concluding our Faith Promise Mission Convention in January following this November report. At our convention, individuals would have the opportunity to make a Faith Promise. A Faith Promise states, "If God provides resources that I do not expect, I will give the following amount to the cause of world missions."

After the convention, I was reviewing the Faith Promise cards. I came across the Faith Promise of a young immigration lawyer in our congregation. He had written as his Faith Promise: The Carmel Conference Center. I was puzzled. We had not spoken of the Carmel Conference Center in any way since the report in November of the previous year.

I called Scott Hicks and asked him what he meant by his faith promise. He stated, "Pastor, you said when we make a Faith Promise, we are partnering with God. Therefore, if I am going to partner with God, I am going to partner for something big."

He then shared that he and his two sons, one three years old and the other five, were praying for the Carmel Conference Center. He said, my five-year-old prays, "God, help us find the money for the Carmel Conference Center," and my three-year-old prays, "God, thank you for the money for the Carmel Conference Center."

I thanked him for sharing with me and for his faith. It was in March that I received a call from Scott. He stated that he had helped an individual immigrant to the U.S. several years ago and the gentleman had succeeded in business and became very wealthy. He then shared that the successful businessman had called him wanting to donate funds to some churches. Scott asked if we had any concrete plans for the Carmel Conference Center. I said, "Scott, it is a 10-year vision. We do not have any drawings." He thought he should share this idea of the Carmel Conference Center with the businessman.

During the conversation, I remembered that Dr. Stephens would be in town the first part of April. I asked Scott if he could schedule a time with his client to meet with Dr. Stephens. He called back a day later and said we can meet. The time was set for later that month when Dr. Stephens would be in town.

The day came for the meeting. I called Scott to confirm the meeting was still on at his office. He replied that it was and then said, "There is something you should know before you arrive. The man you are going to meet is of the Muslim faith." I thanked him for the heads up.

As Sam and I entered Scott's office, I was introduced to a man that towered over me in height at 6'9". I extended my hand to greet him and looked up and said, "Hello, my name is Claude Robold." His hand engulfed my hand, and he replied, "Hello, my name is Muhammed." He then greeted Sam, and Scott asked us to be seated around his office table.

After formalities were finished, Scott asked me to share an overview of the India Gospel League. I had been talking for about five minutes when Muhammed reached in his coat pocket and pulled out a checkbook and pushed it toward Scott and said, "Write a check for $100,000 to these men." Scott pushed the checkbook back toward Muhammed and said, "No, we are not here to ask you for money. I want you to hear about the ministry and give a few days for you to consider and then make a decision if you want to make a gift." Then Scott turned to me and said, "Continue!" Dr. Stephens was emotionally moved and started to stand up to go compose himself. Muhammed asked, "Where are you going? I just want to help men who help God."

So I continued to share about the ministry and the vision of the Carmel Conference Center. Once again Muhammed pushed the checkbook toward Scott and said, "Write a check for $100,000 to these men." Scott replied, "Muhammed, I, as your attorney and you as my client, I am telling you do not write a check today." Muhammed replied, "Scott, I as your client and you as my attorney, I am telling you write a check for $100,000 today."

Scott took the checkbook, filled out the check, and pushed it toward Muhammed to sign. Muhammed signed the check, took it from the checkbook, and handed it to me and said, "Use it where it will do the best good." I said, "Muhammed, you are a generous man. May we pray for you?" Muhammed replied, "You don't need to pray for me. I just want to help men who help God." He then stood, extended his hand to each of us and said, "Goodbye and may God bless you."

Two weeks later, Sam was speaking in a church in New York for their mission's convention. As he shared on Sunday morning, he told the story of Muhammed. After the service the Sr. Pastor and the missions pastor asked to speak with him privately. They inquired as to how much the Carmel Conference Center would cost. Dr. Stephen's shared that the first phase would cost $250,000. The leadership of the congregation made the decision to write a check for $250,000.

Wow! From November to April, a 10-year dream now has the resources to build the first two phases of the Carmel Conference Center. God's resources flow to vision. God is a giver, and He will use channels of his choosing to see that his vision is completed.

Today, the Carmel Conference Center stands fully completed and in full use as a testimony that God's resources flow to vision. If you have a God-given vision; stay true to the vision. God will supply the resources to catapult you to the completion of his vision.

Principle:
God's Resources Flow to Vision

Reflection

- What vision has come to pass and you witnessed God's resources flowing to fulfill that vision?

- What vision has God called you to flow resources into?

- What vision has God challenged you to stay true to until He provides?

"I was not disobedient to the vision from heaven." Acts 26:19

Apply the 3-10-1 method: Read the verse three times, summarize its meaning in 10 words or less, and ask God to reveal one thing He wants to communicate to you.

Dig Deeper: Read the context. Acts 26:12-23

Personal Insights & Reflection

Children Lead
The Way in Giving

The Martin children, Matthew and Nicole, were a wonderful part of the New Covenant Church family. They had been there at the beginning, learning and growing with the other children. It was the season in the church when we were endeavoring to purchase property on which to build our ministry complex.

We had taken the church body on an excursion looking at three different properties. After this Sunday afternoon excursion, with all packing sack lunches and walking several acres of property, it would be in the elders' hands to determine which property would best meet the needs of the congregation and its future.

The site that was chosen was 143.7 acres with two dwellings on the property. The property had been in the Deardorff family for years. A land grant deed had been issued by President Madison, a deed that was still in the owner's possession. The proceeds of the sale of the property would go to build a senior citizens center in the community of Franklin, Ohio.

We had priced property just a quarter of a mile from this farmland. The cost for that property was $15,000 per acre. The price of the farm was $2,500 per acre. As a new congregation, finding financing was difficult. The bank told us if we could provide the first $100,000 up front, they would finance the remaining balance. We had 90 days to raise the $100,000.

This goal was shared with the church, and we decided to have commitment Sunday in 60 days. Everyone was asked to be in prayer as to what God would have them give in the special offering. The 60 days passed rapidly, and the excitement within the church grew high.

We rented a special banquet hall for a commitment Sunday dinner and time of receiving the offering toward the $100,000 goal. The church family had a wonderful time of worship at our rented chapel that morning. We all left the chapel and headed toward the dinner and commitment time.

As the day progressed, there was sharing of the vision for purchasing the property that would become the ministry base for New Covenant Church. Finally, it was time to receive the special offering. Individuals were to come forward and place their offering in specially prepared receptacles. The first two individuals who came forward were the Martin children. They brought their offering directly to me. They each handed me $50 and shared that this was the money they were saving for new bicycles. After asking them if I could share this with the congregation, they gave me their permission. I don't think there was a dry eye in the house at that moment.

The afternoon progressed and over $90,000 was raised in that initial offering. The total would go beyond the $100,000 within two weeks, well within our 90-day goal. The great blessing of experiencing children leading the way in giving, making a sacrificial gift has never left my heart.

Principle:
Little Is Much When God Is in It

Reflection

- How has a child blessed you with their generosity?

- What was the first gift you gave to God as a child?

"Unless you turn and become like little children, you shall not enter the Kingdom of heaven." Matthew 18:3

Apply the 3-10-1 method: Read the verse three times, summarize its meaning in 10 words or less, and ask God to reveal one thing He wants to communicate to you.

Dig Deeper: Read the context. Matthew 18:1-9

Personal Insights & Reflection

Giving Lights the Way

Have you ever received a gift that just seemed to illuminate everything you were facing? It is true that often the gift one gives to another dispels darkness and lights the way for new opportunities.

Such a gift to New Covenant Church literally gave us light. We were in the process of building a new worship auditorium when the general contractor filed for bankruptcy. This was not due to our building project but his own personal difficulties.

His actions immediately struck fear into the sub-contractors as to whether they would receive their compensation. Therefore, several of them withdrew from the project. One of those was the sub-contractor that was to provide all the lighting fixtures for our new building. We were at the point of issuing the order for all the lights needed in the building, but there was no one to move forward to fulfill the needed order.

I recalled that I knew a person in Oklahoma who owned an electrical supply company. I called him and shared our dilemma. He asked for the electrical drawings and told me he would get a bid to me within a few days. True to his word, the bid came within the amount that we expected, and we approved his bid for the job.

All the lighting fixtures arrived on time, and we obtained a local contractor for the installation. As we neared the end of the building project, our administrator shared with me that we had not received an invoice from the company in Oklahoma that had supplied our lighting fixtures. He stated that he had made several contacts with no response. We instructed him to put in escrow the amount that we knew would cover the cost of the lights.

The project was complete, and we were occupying our facility and still no invoice or signing of documents for the cost of the lighting. Then came an important time for me. I had been invited to speak at a series of meetings in a local church in Oilton, Oklahoma. I knew the man who owned the electrical company was a member of the church where I would be speaking. I had an uncomfortable feeling about speaking with this outstanding invoice.

The date came for me to travel to Oilton, Oklahoma. I determined that before I spoke the first time, I would visit the owner of the electrical supply company. As I arrived in Oilton, I immediately made my way to the company office and asked to speak with the owner, David McBride. He graciously welcomed me to the community and told me he was looking forward to the series of meetings.

"David," I said, "I feel uncomfortable because we have not yet received an invoice from you for the lighting of our building project."

"I know," he said, "I know right where the invoice is on my desk, and I am still reviewing to see how much fat we can cut from the invoice." I will get it to you after I have completed that process.

The meeting went well, and the Lord graciously blessed our time in the community. I returned home expecting to soon receive an invoice. Yet several weeks went by and still no invoice. I could not put my mind at ease about this invoice. So, I called David. I asked him about the invoice we had discussed. He responded by saying, "Yes, I have completed the removal of the fat in the invoice, and we find that you do not owe us any payment. Therefore, consider it paid in full."

Once again, the light of Jesus shined through a businessman that was kingdom minded. He would never worship in our building in Ohio, but he had lit the way for many to see and receive the light of the world in Jesus.

Principle:
Light Always Dispels Darkness

Reflection

- Who shared light on your path to Jesus?

- Where and how has God challenged you to be a light in the midst of darkness?

"You are the light of the world. A city on a hill cannot be hidden. In the same way, let your light shine before others, that they may see your good deeds and praise your Father in heaven." Matthew 5:14,16

Apply the 3-10-1 method: Read the verse three times, summarize its meaning in 10 words or less, and ask God to reveal one thing He wants to communicate to you.

Dig Deeper: Read the context. Matthew 5:13-16

Personal Insights & Reflection

The Gift of Care

She is a professor of communication at the local community college. She teaches inmates in local prisons. She is an advocate for those leaving incarceration. She is a giver of care to many.

I first met Heidi Arnold as she was serving her church as chairperson of the pastoral search committee. She was inviting me to become the interim pastor of her local congregation. I could tell right away she was a lady with energy and enthusiasm and poured herself into whatever task she committed to lead.

Perhaps her greatest gift to those she meets is that immediately they know she cares. She cares about others and what she knows she has been called to do. This is demonstrated in her love and care for the elderly in her local congregation.

The congregation has a good number of elderly persons who have lost their spouse, are living alone, and still trying to find purpose for living. I am not sure how she came to lead a group called *Young at Heart*, but these folks are loved by Heidi.

I have often thought the greatest gift you can give is the gift of caring. Heidi really cares for these older adults. She does not get paid for doing this work but does it as unto the Lord. She goes far beyond the causal phone call. Heidi's phone number is on all of their phones and when they call, she answers.

The calls are often taken at inconvenient times and require immediate action. Heidi responds immediately to take someone to the hospital and sit with them until a resolution is found. She takes them to their doctor appointments and returns home with them to set up a proper way for them to remember to take their medication.

She knows each of their birth dates and makes sure they know one another's. She consistently sends cards of recognition and encouragement, plans luncheons, attends funerals, and makes home calls. The elderly of her congregation know they are loved, and they respond to her love.

You do not have to be a scholar, rich or hold a position to give the gift of care. You just need to care about others. Heidi has taken the word of the Lord literally and does unto others as she would have them do unto her. She cares.

Principle:
The Way Others Know You Care
Is to Care

Reflection

- Who has touched your life with care?

- How did they do it?

- What elderly person would know they are not forgotten if you gave the gift of care?

"Share with God's people who are in need. Practice hospitality."
Romans 12:13

Apply the 3-10-1 method: Read the verse three times, summarize its meaning in 10 words or less, and ask God to reveal one thing He wants to communicate to you.

Dig Deeper: Read the context of Romans 12:9-21

Personal Insights & Reflection

The Gift of Compassion

D eath is inevitable. However, when it comes with tragedy, it is almost unbearable. My wife, Jan, was a 17-year-old high school student. The summer of her junior year, she was sharing in her church's Vacation Bible School. During this morning, she was summoned from her classroom to hear the most tragic news of her young life.

Her father, Maurice Rahjes, farmer and entrepreneur had been killed that day in a crop-dusting accident as his plane stalled and crashed to the ground. Jan's grandfather, Gus Rahjes, was the patriarch of a closely knit family who relied upon and supported one another in many ways. But on this day Gus and Blanche Rahjes lost their son; Doyle Rahjes lost his brother; Frances Rahjes lost her husband; and Connie, Janice, Robert and Don Rahjes lost their father in one swift moment.

What is a family to do in such a time of grief? Who comforts who amid such loss? Who fulfills the scripture as a vessel to bring comfort that overflows into the life of another? Does the Lord know our grief and sorrows? Will he provide overflowing comfort?

In the midst of the Rahjes family's darkest hour of grief came a comforting light, an older man that not many of the family knew. He had traveled over 100 miles to stand at the door of the Rahjes home. As they answered his knock, he simply stated he had come to pray with the Rahjes family in their time of grief. He was invited into the home. He audibly prayed over the family, shared his condolences, and left to travel his 100-mile trip home.

Does such an act of compassion make any difference? Sixty years later, this stands out to Jan as one of the greatest acts of kindness given to her family. She remembers at that time there was a presence of comfort and peace.

The gift of true compassion will lead us to do things that call for personal inconvenience. Yet those who are willing to be inconvenienced will bring to others a gift that contains just what the recipient needs in that hour. The gift of compassion is powerful and endures forever.

Principle:

The Gift Offered from a Compassionate Heart Comforts and Soothes a Troubled Soul

Reflection

- Who stepped into your life in a difficult hour with a compassionate heart?

- What does that experience mean to you?

- Who needs the touch of your compassionate heart? How will you share your compassion?

"Carry each other's burdens and in this you will fulfill the law of Christ." Galatians 6:2

Apply the 3-10-1 method: Read the verse three times, summarize its meaning in 10 words or less, and ask God to reveal one thing He wants to communicate to you.

Dig Deeper: Read the context of Galatians 6:1-10

Personal Insights & Reflection

The Presence of One

This was the second major pancreas surgery for my wife. We had journeyed from our home in Ohio to the hospital in Houston, Texas, for this delicate surgery. Our baby daughter was staying with her aunt and our two teen daughters were at home with a friend in Ohio.

A physician friend of mine from Houston had directed us to a surgeon. The day of the surgery came and as Jan was rolled to surgery, I left her bedside to sit in the waiting room alone to await the outcome of this day.

It seemed peculiar that the waiting room was empty, and I was the only one seated in the vast room of uncertainty. About 30 minutes had passed when I sensed a shadow over me. I looked up to see a friend, Pastor John Spear. We had attended college together years ago. He was now the pastor of a church in Pasadena, a neighboring community to Houston.

I still am not aware of how he was aware of Jan's surgery or where it was taking place. It mattered not how he knew; it mattered that he was present. He stayed with me through the hours of waiting to receive the results of the surgery. He left after we had learned of the success of the surgery but what would be a long journey to recovery. Praying with me before he departed, John spoke words of encouragement.

I do not remember the words, but I remember his presence. The gift of presence when one is all alone is a precious gift that leaves an imprint upon your heart for a lifetime. A gift that will cause you to endear that person forever.

Our presence only takes a little effort, but the effort results in a timely gift—the gift of another's concern for your aloneness.

Principle:

The Presence of a Caring Person Extends the Gift of Compassion to One in Need

Reflection

- Who showed up in your time of aloneness to fill the emptiness you were feeling?

- What difference has it made in your life?

- Who do you know that may be standing in a moment of aloneness and your presence would make all the difference at this time?

"An anxious heart weighs a man down, but a kind word cheers him up." Proverbs 12:25

Apply the 3-10-1 method: Read the verse three times, summarize its meaning in 10 words or less, and ask God to reveal one thing He wants to communicate to you.

Dig Deeper: Read the context of Proverbs 12

Personal Insights & Reflection

The Gift of a Mission Heart

Those who have a mission heart have as their purpose to lift others through the blessing of giving. Everyone who knew Chuck and Donna Thomas experienced their mission hearts. After all, they had been at the cutting edge of international missions since the inception of their ministry. They had founded the mission organization known as Project Partner with Christ. They had lifted international Christian leaders all over the world bringing them into partnerships with ministries in the western world.

They encourage Christian leaders in the United States to go into all the world and partner with international Christian leaders, changing and lifting many leaders on both sides of the vast oceans. I would be one of those who experienced a transformation in my life by their encouraging me to meet Rev. Samuel Stephens and join him in ministry to India.

My discovery has been that individuals like Chuck and Donna with a mission heart are consistent with that mission wherever they are called to serve. Chuck and Donna were congregants in two of the churches I pastored. Their mission heart was to lift their pastor in every area of his and his family's life.

Their home was open to us any time of the day, and often when they traveled, they asked us to enjoy their private home, a retreat in the middle in the woods. Their effort to share support in various ways with us was beyond the expectation of any pastor.

Each year for several years, they would take my wife and me and our three daughters for a special Christmas celebration. It would begin with lunch and then a journey to one of the major cities in our area for a Christmas shopping trip. As we would arrive at a particular mall, they would give Jan $1000 and me a $1000 and each of our daughters $500. They would escort us into the mall and say go shopping. The only rule was to spend the entire amount we had been given that day. Naturally this was a tremendous encouragement to Jan and me, but greater still the love it communicated to our daughters was priceless.

The lifting of others comes in many forms: moral support, financial support, and physical support. Being whatever is needed in another person's life is a mission-minded heart. It is the heart of Christ, and when you not only see it in others but experience it directly as a recipient, you are lifted to new levels of giving in your own life.

Principle:
A Mission-Minded Heart Is the Lifter of All It Touches

Reflection

- How were you lifted by an individual with a mission minded heart?

- What transformation hast it brought to your life?

- Who in your path needs a lift from your mission heart?

"The greatest among you should be like the youngest, and the one who rules like the one who serves? Luke 22:26

Apply the 3-10-1 method: Read the verse three times, summarize its meaning in 10 words or less, and ask God to reveal one thing He wants to communicate to you.

Dig Deeper: Read the context of Luke 22:24-30

Personal Insights & Reflection

---→>>>∘⊱··⊰∘<<<←---

Giving Beyond
the Expected

Pastors get all kinds of calls that bring a vast variety of experiences. The call a pastor gets that brings a momentary caution and raises many questions is when a parishioner calls and says, "Pastor, my wife and I want to schedule a meeting with you." I have had several of these kinds of calls; they are not often positive calls. Someone is unhappy about something. Their unhappiness could be with their spouse, their child, the church, a particular ministry, or even the pastor.

On one such occasion I received such a call. The caller immediately responded by saying, "and by the way, Pastor, this is a good meeting." Such was the call from Tom. The day came for him and his wife to meet with me. They were in a jovial mood as they entered my office. Tom began by sharing his appreciation for the church and the ministry of the church. They both shared that they enjoyed the ministries in which they participated.

Tom and his wife had come through a difficult time. Tom had been injured on his job as a fireman, and it had taken a toll on their lives. Tom was forced to take disability leave from his position. But on this day, they were there to share that God had done a miracle for them, and they had just closed on praiseworthy financial success.

As Tom shared this blessing, he slowly pushed an envelope toward me and said, "We want to tithe off of this blessing, and we want the tithe to go to our church." He asked me to open the envelope where inside was a check for $35,000. I rejoiced with them and shared how this would be a blessing to the church. Tom then said, "Pastor, a tithe is what is expected of us, but we want to go beyond the tithe and give an offering. Tom pushed another envelope toward me and enclosed in that envelope was check for $13,000. A total gift of $48,000. This happened to be the exact amount the church was in special need of at that time. Wow, God! You do the unexpected when your children go beyond the expected.

Principle:
Giving Beyond the Expected
Is Giving of Yourself

Reflection
- When in your life have you gone beyond the expected?

- What was the result?

- Where can you move beyond the expected so that you will be God's vessel to accomplish the unexpected?

"You give a tenth of your spices, mint, dill and cumin. But you have neglected the more important matters of the law, justice, mercy, and faithfulness. You should have practiced the latter without neglecting the former." Matthew 23:23

Apply the 3-10-1 method: Read the verse three times, summarize its meaning in 10 words or less, and ask God to reveal one thing He wants to communicate to you.

Dig Deeper: Read the context of Matthew 23:1-36

Personal Insights & Reflection

A Servant Heart Will Change a Negative Perspective

Those who know my wife, Jan, know that her very nature is one of a servant's heart. She has always found joy in serving. She always serves with gladness and with no expectation of any return. Naturally when you serve others there are always blessings in return. One of those blessings is when one who has had a negative perspective of you has that perspective drastically changed by your act of loving and caring service.

Jan has experienced this turn around in a very dramatic way. My mother who grew up under a very difficult mother has suffered from an inferior feeling in many of her adult relationships. She is in no way inferior but old words driven into her mind at a young age have had serious consequences. So, when my mother has had a relationship with someone who has been successful or seems to have more than she has, she struggles with her feelings of inferiority.

Jan grew up on a family farm in Kansas. Her grandfather had established the farm and raised his two sons to be partners in what had become a large wheat and cattle farm. They were very successful because of their work ethic and the blessings of their faith in God.

Jan and I had met in college, and my mother did not have an opportunity to really get acquainted with Jan before we were married. Our wedding was held in Jan's home church in Phillipsburg, Kansas. Naturally, my family was a part of the wedding. When my family arrived at the Rahjes farm and my mother saw what she thought was a family of wealth, her struggle with inferior thoughts began. This led her to have a perspective of Jan as one who she thought was from a family above herself. This, for many years, kept Mom at an emotional distance from Jan.

Then came the day that my mother suffered a stroke that left her incapacitated in many ways. Jan and I knew it was our responsibility to see that Mom got the care she needed. We moved her to our home, and Jan became Mom's caregiver in the most intimate of matters.

Yes, Jan began to serve my mother with her loving and servant heart. This led my mother into a major transformation in her relationship with Jan. She was seeing Jan for who she really is rather than from her misconceived perception. I can tell you it has changed my mother in many ways for the good in these later years of her life. It has proven to me that a servant heart will change a negative perspective.

Principle:

A Servant Heart Can Change
a Negative Perspective
in Another Individual

Reflection

- What negative perspective was changed because you served with the grace of a servant heart?

- What difference did it make?

- Who misunderstands the real you?

- How could you serve them and change that negative perspective?

"Do not use your freedom to indulge in the sinful nature; rather, serve one another in love." Galatians 5:13b

<u>Apply the 3-10-1 method:</u> Read the verse three times, summarize its meaning in 10 words or less, and ask God to reveal one thing He wants to communicate to you.

<u>Dig Deeper:</u> Read the context of Galatians 5:1-15

Personal Insights & Reflection

The Gift of Sacrifice

Someone had to give a sacrificial gift for us to enjoy the life we live today. Many have given their lives in military duty to defend the freedom we experience every day. Our mothers made many sacrifices just to bring us into this world. You may be one of those blessed individuals who can acknowledge a special sacrifice someone made in your behalf to enhance or even save your life.

It is important for us to know that if we are to live lives of joyful giving and living, we will be called upon to make a sacrificial gift at some point in our life to be a special blessing in the life of another person. How can we prepare for such a time? How can we have the mindset so we can readily say yes to sacrificial giving?

We can begin by accepting the sacrificial gift given for every one of us. Sacrificial giving must start with a commitment to live a life of love for others. The Holy Scriptures tell us this recorded in the little epistle of I John 3:16-17. "This is how we know what love is: Jesus

Christ laid down his life for us. And we ought to lay down our lives for one another."

How do you accept this kind of love? Why should you accept this kind of love, this sacrificial gift of love? Let us respond to each of these questions. The first step is to recognize that we all are seeking such a love. We were created to be loved and agents of love. It is this love that brings redemption expressing how much God values each of us; therefore, I accept this gift as a basic need in my life. Second, I must come to believe that I am loved. There are many negative experiences that come into our lives that we allow to negate this truth. The great teacher, Apostle Paul, wrote that while we were unlovable, Christ died for us. The good news is God loves the world and has made a sacrificial gift to demonstrate that love in dying for us to pay the ransom of that which separates us from him. Third, we must allow God to change our hearts to be filled with his love so we can love one another sacrificially. Today, simply say to God, I receive your gift of sacrificial love. Thank you for loving me and taking the penalty of my transgressions. Fill me with your love and allow your love to live through me touching others with this transforming sacrificial love.

Principle:
Sacrificial Love Is the Greatest Gift One Could Ever Offer Another

Reflection

- Reflect upon the moment your realized you were loved by God.

- Who did God use to bring you to that awareness?

- How did it happen?

- How will I live and continue to grow in that love so that I can love another in the same way?

"For God so loved the world that he gave his one and only son, that whosoever believes in him shall not perish but have eternal life." John 3:16

Apply the 3-10-1 method: Read the verse three times, summarize its meaning in 10 words or less, and ask God to reveal one thing He wants to communicate to you.

Dig Deeper: Read the context of John 3:1-21

Personal Insights & Reflection

Epilogue

I have discovered a serendipity in the writing of this book. I wonder if that is not the experience of every author. As you are writing and researching, there comes that wonderful moment that affirms the subject you are writing about.

This was my experience as I endeavored to reconnect with the artist that created the picture on the cover of this book. I had last seen the artist I knew as Sherry O'Bryan in 1980. I was living in Modesto, California, when she gave me the hand-drawn art with an encouraging inscription. All these years later, in thinking about the cover for this book, I immediately knew this would be it. So, I began the journey of trying to find Sherry.

I was not having very much success when I remembered my colleague Shirley Roddy had been a dear friend to Sherry. Shirley had lived in Modesto but later in life moved to Oklahoma City where she went on to earn her Ph.D. Much of her work was done in research. I thought if anyone can find Sherry, it will be Shirley. When I called, Shirley gladly agreed to help in my search.

Within a few days, I received a call from Shirley with the contact information for Sherry. Shirley stated, "She is anticipating your call, and she has a great story to share with you." I could hardly wait to contact Sherry and get her permission to use the drawing for this book. After a few moments of reconnection, I asked if she remembered the drawing. She reminded me that I had used the drawing to be the front on a series of thank you cards. I had sent her one of the cards with a message of appreciation for her gift of art to the daycare which our church operated. She then said, "I still have that thank you card."

She readily gave me permission to use it for the cover of this book. Then she said, "I need to tell you a story."

When you knew me, I was married and a very young mother. I had dropped out of high school and was working as a waitress in a local restaurant. I had my young son in your church daycare. I was so blessed by the care he was given and the warmth of the director, Shirley Roddy, that I started attending the North Modesto Church of God.

I had run into a rough patch, and on one occasion, I could not pay the bill at the daycare. Shirley Roddy, the director, said let's find a way to help you. She knew that I was an artist and said if I would paint murals on the walls for the children, they would receive that as payment for my childcare debt. So, I was standing on a ladder painting in one of the rooms one day when Shirley entered the room. She stood watching me for a while and then standing with her hands on her hips she said, "Sherry, how would you like to work with children?" She could have not said anything that would have touched my heart any deeper.

Shirley began to work with me to get my GED and then encouraged me to go to the local community college and take classes on early childhood education. This began a journey of me going on to complete my college degree in education, and for many years, I have been a teacher in our local schools. My husband passed away, and my name in now Cheryl Swart.

Can you believe that one statement of encouragement could change the trajectory of an entire life?

That is the serendipity that comes to individuals who are willing to give to others. Did Shirley know that one simple question would change the path of Cheryl's life? I doubt that was her first thought, but when you are a giver like Shirley, that is the gift you get in return.

I have found that one of the most profound gifts a person can give is a word of encouragement. When we are willing to give the gift of encouragement, we instill and stir up courage in another individual that can change their life for the positive forever.

That could be the subject for my next book.

Blessings,
Claude Robold

Resource Recommendations

Bobb Biehl
Executive Mentor and Consultant
Provides a vast array of excellent leadership material
At Bobbbiehl.com
DECADE BY DECADE
Available at SeedPlanter.net

Professor Heidi Arnold
Provides an insightful writing in her book
BELLY FULL OF STONES
Available on Amazon

Kathy Crockett
Executive Entrepreneur
Provides words of encouragement in her books
COURAGEEOUS MEN AND WOMEN OF FAITH
Available on Amazon

Rev. Steve Childs
Provides wisdom in his writings
DAILY DEVOTIONALS
Available at SEChilds@aol.com

Dr. Sam Bruce
Provides an excellent guide to Spiritual Formation
SPIRITUAL FORMATION
Available on Amazon

About the Author

Claude Robold served over 50 years in pastoral ministry. He also served as a strategic planning consultant for nonprofit organizations. He served 13 years as chairman of Mid-America Christian University. He has served as a special speaker in many venues around the world.

He is the father of three daughters and the grandfather of seven wonderful grandchildren. He and his wife Janice of 57 years live in Middletown, Ohio.

Made in the USA
Columbia, SC
23 March 2023

14084393R00064